Ex-miner Max Boyce is one of the nicest people you could hope to meet. He thundered to national success with his first album, *Live at Treorchy*, though he had already won a huge reputation by singing in village halls and rugby clubs throughout Wales. All Max Boyce's songs, whether delivered with a grin and wicked twinkle in the eye, or with deeply serious intentions, stem from his roots and experience of the community in which he was born and still lives. Fellow Welshmen will recognize themselves in the lyrics with shame and pleasure. For non-Welshmen, the songs and poems – funny, sad, lyrical and always inventive – are a revelation.

*Max Boyce*

# Max Boyce:

## His Songs and Poems

*Introduction by Barry John*

*Cartoons by Gren*

PANTHER
**GRANADA PUBLISHING**
London Toronto Sydney New York

Published by Granada Publishing Limited
in Panther Books 1976
Reprinted 1977, 1978 (twice), 1979, 1980

ISBN 0 586 04621 6

A Panther Original


Granada Publishing Limited
Frogmore, St Albans, Herts AL2 2NF
and
3 Upper James Street, London W1R 4BP
866 United Nations Plaza, New York, NY10017, USA
117 York Street, Sydney, NSW 2000, Australia
100 Skyway Avenue, Rexdale, Ontario, M9W 3A6, Canada
PO Box 84165, Greenside, 2034 Johannesburg, South Africa
CML Centre, Queen & Wyndham, Auckland 1, New Zealand

Made and printed in Great Britain by
Richard Clay (The Chaucer Press) Ltd
Bungay, Suffolk
Set in Linotype Baskerville

# Contents

# Introduction

If you don't like rugby; or singing; or Welshmen; then this book probably isn't for you – but don't go looking for sympathy for your bad taste.

There are those (probably in the pay of the England Selection Committee) who might disagree if I said that Max Boyce was the greatest living Welshman; mind you, Max would probably disagree as well – but there's no other living man who's composed a song regularly sung at Cardiff Arms Park alongside *Cwm Rhondda* and *Sospan Fach*.

Who is Max Boyce, then? He's been described in a lot of ways – the Welsh singer-comedian, the Welsh Billy Connolly, a Welsh folk hero – but none of these really do him justice. Max once said that the two main influences on him were Dylan Thomas and Al Read, but when you listen to his songs you realize the real influence is the world he grew up in – South Wales.

Max Boyce comes from Glyn Neath, a small town between Swansea and Merthyr Tydfil. He still lives there in a small house in a terraced street. His father was a miner; he was killed underground the month Max was born. Max spent eight years on the shifts in the mines before his success allowed him to get out.

He started singing at a folk club in Pontardawe, performing a song he'd written himself. He wrote more songs, got himself well-known in the clubs in Wales, then went on 'Opportunity Knocks'. He won a silver medal, but he still thinks it was the biggest mistake he made; later, when he was a success, he told a reporter from the *Guardian*:

> They don't like silver medals in Wales ... You'd think I'd come last, not second. But you don't come back here

with a silver medal. If you're competing for Wales, then you win.

But it was only a setback, and it made him fight all the harder. It was when he was part of the supporting bill for Harry Secombe at Swansea that EMI spotted him. That led to the legendary 'Live at Treorchy' (Treorchy Rugby Club, that is) LP. It contained some of his classic songs – 'Morgan the Moon', 'The Outside-Half Factory', 'Duw It's Hard' and, of course, 'Hymns and Arias'. 'Live at Treorchy' pretty soon became a sell-out. It was followed by TV appearances (on the 'Poets and Pints' series) and a growing reputation in England. The night before an England–Wales match at Twickenham he played to a crowd of 2,000 at the New Victoria. Last St David's Day he did a nine-minute spot at the Albert Hall, singing for 6,000 people: and he returned there in October, topping the bill. His last LP went to Number 1, giving him his second Gold disc. Max Boyce is a star.

But he's a star without ballyhoo or glitter. The essence of Max Boyce is captured on the cover of 'Live at Treorchy'. He's a dark, curly-haired man, with a wicked grin. He wears a shabby raincoat decorated with a huge rosette and a leek. He's in a rugby club with a pint of beer on the table in front of him.

It's the same with his songs. Tin Pan Alley had nothing to do with Max Boyce's success. He's not a manufactured product with a characterless appeal that works the same from Los Angeles to London. His songs come directly from his own world and they speak directly to the people who live there. They're about the things that are part of life in South Wales: rugby, singing and, of course, coal mining. Max has tried all of them and they're all there in his songs.

If you listen to his LPs, the first thing that you notice about Max Boyce is the rapport he has with his audience. He's a natural comedian with a totally Welsh sense of humour and a way of laughing *with* his audience – never at them. His hilarious story of his first appearance at an Eisteddfod, when his mother, his aunties and uncles and his cousin, all saw him failing to recite 'The Squirrel' could only happen in Wales. He talks about things his audience know – the Treorchy team, Dai Morris carved out of rock, the trip up to 'Twickers' to see the Welsh team defeat the English. It's not really parochial, though; it's a humour that belongs to a community, but London audiences find it just as funny. Max's sense of timing is fantastic, for one thing – his pauses are sometimes as funny as his punchlines. He's at his best on his own territory, a Welsh rugby club – but that didn't stop him taking the Albert Hall by storm.

Then there are the songs. The rugby ones first, of course. Rugby's not just a sport in Wales, it's a way of life, a national pastime, even a religion. And in rugby, your first loyalty is to your local club; and then to the Welsh team against all comers (and one in particular). Max Boyce is rugby's great songwriter. His songs are about every aspect of rugby: legendary victories, like the time Llanelli beat the All Blacks (Seland Newydd) at Stradey Park, 9–3 (which is also the title of the song) or the time a Japanese touring team came to Wales; famous players like the Pontypool Front Row; and those wonderful coach outings to Scotland or Twickenham. He sings about the tragedy of not having a ticket for the Seland Newydd match:

*They poured down from the valleys,*
*they came from far and wide;*
*There were 20,000 in the ground*
*and me and Dai outside.*

and of the lengths men will go to get to a match:

*We all had doctors' papers,*
*Not one of us in pain,*
*And Harry Morgan buried*
*His granny once again.*

Then there's the remarkable story of how the Welsh supporters descended on London for the International and the terrible thing that was done with a bottle that had once held bitter ale; that song's called 'Hymns and Arias', incidentally, and it's the one the Welsh crowd sings these days.
And there's his marvellously zany fantasy, 'The Outside-Half Factory', about a mine hidden in a Welsh valley where they dig out 'the most priceless commodity known to Welshmen' from 'a four foot seam of outside halves two miles below the ground'.

*My Dad works down in Arms and Legs*
*Where production's running high;*
*It's he that checks the wooden moulds*
*And stacks them 40 high.*
*But he's had some rejects lately*
*'Cos there's such a big demand,*
*So he sells them to the Northern Clubs*
*And stamps them 'Second Hand'*

There's more to life than rugby, though – there's singing as well and ninety minutes of roaring and singing leave a man thirsty; and it's just as well to wet the throat beforehand. Victory, of course, needs celebrating; and defeat brings sorrow to be drowned. Beer is part of the atmosphere of rugby – and of Max's records. He may exaggerate a little sometimes, but who could fail to be moved by the fate of poor Will in 'The Scottish Trip', or by this sad story of what happened after the Seland Newydd match:

*I saw a grown man cry*
*Not because we'd won –*
*but because the pubs ran dry.*

But there's a serious side to Max Boyce as well. He was brought up in a part of our world which has known more hard times than most; and for eight years he worked as a miner, a cruel and dangerous job which has claimed many lives. One of his finest songs, 'Duw It's Hard', tells of the closing of a pit. The miners aren't sad, even though 'the pithead bath is a supermarket now': you don't mourn a dangerous and dirty mine. But there's still resentment towards those who make the decisions, with their

*briefcases full of bankclerks*
*that have never been below*

because they'll never understand what it's like in the mines. That's also the message of the song Max wrote about the miners' strike – 'Did You Understand?' – when the miners were being judged and condemned by people who couldn't understand. Max Boyce understands: as he says, every time he coughs he gets 'a mining souvenir'.

Through all Max Boyce's songs runs a pride and love for Wales. On 'We All Had Doctors' Papers' he sings a beautiful version of the traditional song 'A'r Lan Y Mor', but elsewhere he combines a fierce pride in Wales with a whimsical humour. Did you know, for instance, that the first man on the moon was a Welshman? All the Americans did was to bring their man back. Morgan the Moon's still there with his coal-powered rocket, 'Bethania'. After that, it comes as no surprise to learn that even in Heaven the Welsh have got the best rugby team, while the English are struggling to get a Fifteen together. The English appear quite often in these songs. They're villains to a man, but the humour directed at them is never cruel. The lances are not barbed, there is no bitterness.

Max Boyce embodies Welshness better than any one I know: he has the wry humour, the passion, the music and the melancholy which only exist in that combination in Wales. It's good to see him gaining recognition so widely, and to think that a lot of people who've never heard Welsh humour at its best will get a chance to find out what they're missing. But I don't think there's any danger of Wales losing Max Boyce; however many London papers print articles about him, and however often he plays the Albert Hall (and may every time be the night before a Welsh victory), his roots and his home are firmly in Wales, with the people he knows and within reach of a rugby club.

If you haven't heard him, I hope it won't be too long before you do. There are so many moments to treasure in his songs: like his hysterical parody of 'Deck of Cards', where the bible is replaced by the Rugby Union handbook; or the council workmen singing Happy Birthday to their hole 'because it's one year old today'. He creates an absolutely crazy, absolutely real world full of larger-than-life characters with only two things on their minds. But if you doubt their existence, take a trip to South Wales; or if you can't do that, go to Twickenham when England and Wales are playing. That's Max Boyce's world; and he's its greatest entertainer.

Barry John

# The Pontypool Front Row

by Max Boyce

Now I'll tell you all a story
About some lads I know.
Who're known throughout the valleys
As the Pontypool Front Row.
It's got a little chorus
And that chorus you all know.
So tell me are you ready?
Up-and-under here we go!

CHORUS
Up-and-under, here we go.
Are you ready, yes or no?
Up-and-under here we go:
It's the song of the Pontypool Front Row.

Now they made a film in London,
It was censored double-X.
The sort of film that frightens one,
Not one of lust and sex.
Mary Whitehouse saw it
And now they'll never show
A film called 'Up-and-Under'
Starring the Pontypool Front Row!

We had trouble in Uganda
With President Amin.
So they sent an envoy out there
With a message from the Queen.
To stay that execution
But Amin answered 'No!'
Till a card was sent from the Viet Gwent –
The Pontypool Front Row!

They've had trouble on the railways
With some of soccer's fans.
I've seen them on the terraces
Throwing stones and cans.
They've stopped the soccer specials,
It's a waste of time I know.
'Cos in the end they'll have to send
For the Pontypool Front Row!

There's a programme on the telly –
I watch it when I can –
The story of an astronaut,
The first bionic man.
He cost six million dollars –
That's a lot of bread I know
But Wigan offered more than that
For the Pontypool Front Row!

# Swansea Town

by John Davies & Billy Jewell
(Additional lyric by Max Boyce)

I'm going home to Swansea Town:
The day is nearly dawning.
I'm going home to the seaport sound
One lovely seatown morning.

I'm going home to Swansea Town:
To where the ways are brambled.
Neath the seatown sky where seagulls cry
Where as a boy I rambled.

And she'll be waiting there for me;
She'll be glad to see me.
And I'll not leave my town again;
A fortune won't persuade me.

I'm going home to Swansea Town:
The day is nearly dawning.
I'm going home to the seaport sound
One lovely seatown morning.
One lovely seatown morning.

# I Gave My Love a Debenture

by Max Boyce

I met her in the Con. Club in Pontypool;
The public bar was crowded so I offered her my stool.
I said 'Fair lass, pray tarry. Come stay awhile with me.
And I'll give you my debenture – Block A, Row 3.

Her eyes were pale as lyder; her hair was long and
black.
The only thing that spoiled her was she wore a plastic
mac.
I said 'Fair lass, pray tarry. Come sit upon my knee.'
She thought awhile and then she smiled. I thought
'Ho, ho, he, he, hee hee hee!'

She said she came from Crumlin and that her name
was Ann.
She told me 'You can walk me home.' I said 'I've got a
van!'
We turned into a lay-by, where she told me she loved
me.
So I gave her my debenture – Block A, Row 3.

That night I met her mother. (She was waiting for us
there.)
Stockings round her ankles and curlers in her hair.
She was waiting on the doorstep, and she waved her
fist at me.
So I showed her my debenture – Block A, Row 3.

That night when I was sleeping my love proved false
to me;
And left me for another who's known as * * G.
I know I'll not forget her for she was the rue of me;
And she's got my debenture – Block A, Row 3.

*'I gave my love a debenture ...'*

So take my warning all you lads, for girls the likes
of she.
They only want you for one thing – your debenture
in Row 3!
So should you go to Crumlin, pray tread the night
with care:
Take heed I pray and stay away from that girl with
the long black hair.

# I Am an Entertainer

by Max Boyce

I am an entertainer and I sing for charity:
For Oxfam and for Shelter, for those worse off than me.
Bangla Desh, Barnardo's Homes. And though I don't
get paid,
It does one good to do some work
For things like Christian Aid.

But of all the concerts that I've done for the homeless
overseas,
The one I did that pleased me most was not for
refugees.
'Twas for a home in Ireland that stands amongst the
trees:
The sunshine home in Dublin for blind Irish referees!

# The Devil's Marking Me

by Max Boyce

I had a dream the other night,
The strangest dream of all.
I dreamt I was in Heaven,
Away from life's hard call.
It was as I'd imagined –
Where peace ruled all serene.
The signs to Heaven were all in Welsh:]
Hell's signs were painted green!

    Painted green, painted green.
    The signs to Heaven were all in Welsh:]
    Hell's signs were painted green.

I entered through the heavenly gate,
I heard the heavenly band.
And there was John the Baptist
On Barry John's right hand!
He plays for the Heaven Welsh XV –
They're very fit and keen.
We'd play the Heaven English
If they could only raise a team!

    Raise a team, raise a team.
    We'd play the Heaven English
    If they could only raise a team.

There was Rugby every morning
On a field of golden corn.
And the referee was Gabriel
And he blew on a silver horn.
They tell me we play Hell next week
In the annual charity.
I wouldn't mind but I've been told
The devil's marking me!

Marking me, marking me.
I wouldn't mind but I've been told
The devil's marking me.

But now my dream has faded
And I wake up to the morn.
I find beneath my pillow
A sheaf of golden corn.
So I know that when I go there,
Beyond death's victory,
I'll take my Rugby jersey
On that Gospel train with me.

Train with me, train with me.
I'll take my Rugby jersey
On that Gospel train with me.
Train with me, train with me.
I'll take my Rugby jersey
On that Gospel train with me.

# Deck of Cards

by T. Texas Tyler
New Lyric by Max Boyce

During the latter part of last season, a bunch of students had been on a long sponsored walk. They arrived in a little town called Ystrad.

The next day being Tuesday, some of the boys went training. A Welsh Rugby Union coach commanded the boys in training, and after he had outlined various scrummaging techniques, he told them to take out their Welsh Rugby Union handbook.

Those of the boys who had Welsh Rugby Union handbooks, took them out. But one boy had only a Deck of Cards, and so he spread them out.

The coach saw the cards and said 'Boy, put away those cards!' After the training session was over the boy was taken away, and taken in front of the Welsh Rugby Union.

And Bill Clement said: 'Why have you brought this boy here?'

'For playing cards in a training session, sir.'

'And what have you to say for yourself, son?'

'Much, sir!'

And Bill Clement said 'I hope so. For if you haven't I will punish you more severely than any boy was ever punished.'

The boy said 'Sir, I have been away in college for six months and had with me neither Welsh Rugby Union handbook or my Ray Williams coaching leaflets!

'But I hope to satisfy you, sir, with the purity of my intentions.'

And with that the boy began his story:

'You see sir, when I look at the ace, it reminds me there is but one game – Rugby Football! And the ace also reminds me of Eddie Waring when he goes "Eh, eh, it's

'Deck of Cards parody'

an up-and-under."

When I see the two, it reminds me that there are two codes of Rugby, Rugby Union and * * !

When I see the trey, I think of the Viet Gwent – the Pontypool Front Row. Charlie Faulkner, Bobby Windsor and Graham Price.

When I see the four, it reminds me of the four Home Countries: Wales, Scotland, Ireland and ???????.

When I see the five, I think of the big five: three were wise and picked Dai – and two were foolish and picked Cobner!

When I see the six of course I think of Dai Morris.

When I see the seven, I think of the Snelling Sevens at the end of each season.

When I see the eight I think of the great Mervyn Davies, the greatest "number eight" in the world.

And of course when I see the nine I think of – Gareth Edwards? No, Dai Morris upside-down!

When I see the ten it reminds me of the years I worked in the Outside-Half Factory, producing that self-same number ten.

When I see the jack, or the knave, or the devil I think of the Rugby League scouts.

When I see the queen I think of Her Majesty Queen Elizabeth, who bestowed on the great Gareth Edwards the MBE. (Some people will do anything for tickets!)

When I see the king, it reminds me of the player they once called "the king" – Barry John.

When I count the number of spots on my deck of cards I find 365 – the number of points we've scored against England in the last couple of games at Cardiff!

There are 52 cards in a pack: the number of people who come and see Pontardulais on Saturdays!

There are four suits: the number of weeks in a month.

There are twelve picture cards: the number of times Wales have won the Triple Crown.

There are thirteen tricks: the number of times they'll have won it by this time next year!

So you see, sir, my pack of cards serves me not only as an almanac but as a Welsh Rugby Union handbook.

And friends, that story is true. I know, 'cos I was that boy!'

# At the Bottom of the Garden

by Max Boyce

At the bottom of the garden there's a place you all know,
Where everybody hurries but they try not to show.
Though colliers and lawyers and J.Ps and earls:
Teachers and preachers and young boys and girls.

CHORUS
Singing Toora-ly, oora-ly, oora-ly, ay.
Have you been down there – my darlings, today?
Where there ain't any telly and there isn't a phone:
Where even the King has to go on his own!

They can have their fine mansions and their ivory walls;
They can have their stained windows and echoey halls.
But I'll never be envious although I'm alone:
I'm happy to sit on my own little throne.

Now the people from Cardiff, they spend quite a lot
To try and disguise what, like us, they have got.
There's lace on the curtains and they've Marleyed the floor!
But the plumbing's disconnected – it's just there for show.

But the people from Ponty have theirs designed
So they can sit there with their hands entwined!
And the green lawn around it is perfectly mown,
But the writing on the wall, damn, it can't be their own.

Now the country today's in a terrible way,
With the chapels and churches not paying their way.
But there's one little place that I really can say
It's as popular now as it was yesterday.

Singing toora-ly, oora-ly, oora-ly, ay.
Oora-ly, oora-ly, oora-ly, ay.
There's more to my song but must be on my way,
I haven't been down there, my darlings, today!

# Green Green Fields

by Max Boyce

Now it's never been the same
Since that news from London came:
Games are cancelled now but not for any rain.
Down Bont Road I look with tears a-falling,
Cos I can see bulldozers crawling,
Why can't they leave our Green Green Field alone?
    But they'll bring that ugly concrete highway,
    To take away what once was my way.
    Why can't they leave our Green Green Field alone?

The old Club House is still standing,
Though the paint is cracked and dry.
And there's that one-armed-bandit that we used to play
    on.
Down that road I look with tears a-falling,
'Cos I can see a Euclid crawling.
Why can't they leave our Green Green Field alone?

But as I bat and look around me
At the four short legs that surround me,
I realize that surveyor wasn't joking.
'Cos this spiny heartless concrete highway
Will take away what once was my way.
Why can't they leave our Green Green Field alone?
    But they'll bring that ugly concrete highway
    To take away what once was my way.
    Why can't they leave our Green Green Field alone?

They have thundered through the hills,
Past the streams and watermills.
They have turned our little valley floor to stone.
They have broken through the farms and churches,
Lovely oaks and silver birches.
Why can't they leave our Green Green Field alone?
    But we'll fight although we ain't got money,
    (I've got a Butty in the Free Wales Army!)
    Why can't they leave our Green Green Field alone.

# Trading Stamps

by Max Boyce

Now my mother shops down at the corner,
Where there's worms and there's germs on his ham.
There's muck on the floor as you walk through the door,
But there's treble the stamps on the jam!

CHORUS:
I've been spending, not saving my money,
Which is why I am poorly shod.
I'm spending not saving my money,
Aye on double and treble and quad.

Now my 57 books bought a mower:
It had seat-belts, a brake and a horn.
Now I'm saving like mad for 57 more –
Going to buy my new mower a lawn!

I've been saving for fourteen long years now,
And I've got ten thousand or more.
I've nearly enough for a colour TV,
Only ten and a half million more!

But when I die and I ascend up to Heaven,
St Peter will meet me and laugh.
He will say 'I am sorry, I can't let you in:
You've only got a book and a half!'

# The Ballad of Morgan the Moon

by Max Boyce

Old Mog the mechanic, I remember him well.
He once built a rocket, or so they will tell.
From an old winding-engine he found on the dole –
Built in the Rhondda and powered by coal.
  Sing fal-da-ral, dal-da-ral day!

And when it was finished he painted it red,
And he called it 'Bethania', or so it is said.
And he took it up a mountain on a night late in June
'To get that bit closer,' said Morgan the Moon.
  Sing fal-da-ral, dal-da-ral day!

Sleepy Treorchy was bathed in white light
When the shuddering hulk took off in the night.
A deafening scream and then a great roar,
And up past the houses old Morgan did go.
  Sing fal-da-ral, dal-da-ral day!

His heat-shield was glowing like anthracite coal
And we prayed down in Cardiff, in mission control.
The barrow-wheels dropped as was previously planned
And old Morgan prepared for Bethania to land.
  Sing fal-da-ral, dal-da-ral day!

He landed like linen on a crusty old crater:
Dai said he'd get there lunar or later!
So off Morgan went in the moon's swirling dust,
To collect some rock samples from a crater's hard crust.
  Sing fal-da-ral, dal-da-ral day!

*'Morgan the Moon'*

A strange piece of rock soon old Morgan found,
Just lying there shining on the dust-covered ground.
He picked it up closely and he let out a call
'Cos written right through it in Welsh was 'Porthcawl'!
Sing fal-da-ral, dal-da-ral day!

# 9–3

by Max Boyce

It was on a dark and dismal day
In a week that had seen rain,
When all roads led to Stradey Park
With the All-Blacks here again.
They poured down from the valleys,
They came from far and wide;
There were twenty-thousand in the ground
And me and Dai outside!

The shops were closed like Sunday,
And the streets were silent still.
And those who chose to stay away
Were either dead or ill.
But those who went to Stradey, boys,
Will remember till they die
How New Zealand were defeated,
And how the pubs ran dry.

Oh, the beer flowed at Stradey
(Piped down from Felinfoel),
And the hands that held the glasses high
Were strong from steel and coal.
And the air was filled with singing,
And I saw a grown man cry.
Not because we'd won
But because the pubs ran dry!

Then dawned the morning after
On empty factories.
But we were still at Stradey –
Bloodshot absentees.
But we all had doctors' papers
And they all said just the same:
That we all had scarlet fever,
And we caught it at the game!

Now all the little babies
In Llanelli from now on
Will be christened Ray or Carwyn,
Derek, Delme, Phil or John.
And in a hundred years again
They'll sing this song for me.
Of when the scoreboard read 'Llanelli 9,
Seland Newydd 3'.

And when I'm old and my hair turns grey,
And they put me in a chair,
I'll tell my great-grandchildren
That their tad-cu was there.
And they'll ask to hear the story
Of that damp October day,
When I went down to Stradey
And I saw the scarlets play.

# Did You Understand?

by Max Boyce

I remember the time of the collier and the candle,
Of a long bitter fight that darkened the land.
And I asked you the question but you wouldn't answer:
When I asked you the question did you understand?
Collier laddie, collier boy.

I saw mills and machines, all lying there idle;
A million or more unemployed in the land.
And I asked them the question but they wouldn't answer:
When I asked them the question did they understand?
Collier laddie, collier boy.

Then I saw the ones sit in the seats of decision;
They sat and they judged the miners' demand.
And they all heard the case of the lowly-paid miner:
But though they decided, did they understand?
Collier laddie, collier boy.

Then I saw an old collier, whose body lies broken,
Claimed by the dust much finer than sand.
And I asked him the question, though now he can't
answer:
I'll ask him the question he'll understand.
Collier laddie, collier boy.

*Did you understand?*

# Asso Asso Yogoshi

by Max Boyce

We play Wales on Lugby tour,
It long way from Tokyo.
Learn 'Cŵm Rhondda' if we can:
Teach to little children in Japan.

CHORUS:
Asso asso yogoshi;
Me Welsh-speaking Japanese.

In Penyglaig we play first game:
Papers say we not to blame.
Gareth Edwards got velly long pass
But not as long as Penygraig grass!

Western Mail say we too small:
We can't get no ball at all.
But we eat bamboo shoots to grow:
Fit platform boots to second row!

But we build big new factorlies,
Filled with plastic surgeries.
Next time we come you no laugh:
We have nine-foot outside half!

Next time we come from Japan
We'll have velly, velly seclet plan.
Seclet plan, man, we can't wait:
Kung Fu he train to be number eight!

Tommy David, he velly big man:
None like him out in Japan.
But when we found we couldn't stop
We give him ** karate chop.

*'Tommy David velly big man, none like him – out in Japan'*
(ASSO ASSO YOGOSHI)

When we lost we did not flown:
Geisha girls will lub us down.
Gareth Edwards asked me, please,
Next time can he play for Japanese!

So me buy plesent if I can
For wife back home out in Japan.
She opened box, find something long:
Little Welsh doll made in Hong Kong!

# The Scottish Trip

by Max Boyce

Oh we went up to the Hielands of Scotland,
To the land of the loch and the glen.
And we'll all bring our wives back a present
So we can go next time again!

CHORUS:
Too-ral-ay, oo-ral-ay, addy.
We went up by train and by car.
When the juice of the barley starts flowing
We all saw the game in the bar.

Oh we loaded the bus up with flagons,
And we left about twenty past seven.
We stopped fourteen times between Neath and
Bridgend:
We were still in Glamorgan at eleven.

On the M5 Will spoke to the driver,
He said 'Can you no stop this bus for a while?'
He said 'Man alive, we're on the M5.
You'll have to hang on till Carlisle'.

Old Willie climbed out on the sun-roof
And he stood on the bus in disgrace.
But he wasn't to know that that bridge was so low,
But he died with a smile on his face!

He was splattered all over the pavement,
And his leek, it was stuffed down his throat.
And I heard his friend say as they scraped Will away
'My ticket was inside his coat'!

*'And we were singing, Hymns and Arias . . .'*

# The Outside-half Factory

by Max Boyce

I'll tell you all a story, 'tis a strange and a weird tale:
Of a factory in my valley, not fed by road or rail.
It's built beneath the mountain, beneath the coal and clay.
It's where we make the outside-halves, that'll play for Wales one day.

Down by the council houses, where on a quiet day
You can hear the giant engines digging up the clay.
No naked lights or matches where the raw material's found
In the four-foot seams of outside-halves, two miles below the ground.

We've camouflaged the mouth with stones, from Bradford Northern spies:
From plastic 'E-Type' Englishmen with promise in their eyes.
And we've boarded up the entrance for the way must not be shown;
And we'll tell them all to *** off and make their *** own!

My Dad works down in arms and legs where production's running high.
It's he that checks the wooden moulds and stacks them forty high.
But he's had some rejects lately, 'cos there's such a big demand;
So he sells them to the northern clubs, and stamps them 'second-hand'.

It's there where Harry Dampers works, it's where the money's best,
But now his health is failing and the dust lies on his chest.
But he'll get his compensation though his health's gone off the rails
When he sees that finished product score the winning try for Wales.

But now the belts are empty, came a sadness with the dawn.
And the body-press is idle, and the valley's blinds are drawn.
Disaster struck this morning when a fitter's mate named Ron
Cracked the mould of solid gold, that once made Barry John.

Old Harry Dampers (struck with grief), received the final call.
And old Harry has been taken to the greatest outside-half of all.
Whose hands are kind and gentle, though they bear the mark of nails,
So Harry stamped him 'Number Ten', 'cos he was made in Wales.

And the wheels will go on turning, and trams will run on rails,
To that factory 'neath the mountain making outside-halves for Wales.

# Ten Thousand Instant Christians

by Max Boyce

When He sees the 'Hope & Anchor' where we sang before the game,
Where 'Cŵm Rhondda' and 'Delilah' first sounded both the same.
The bar was filled with singing, and the songs came on a tray.
Saturday was Sunday, I wonder what He'll say?

CHORUS:
What will He say?
What will He say?
I wonder, I wonder what He'll say.

When He sees the North Enclosure with its belly-full of ale,
And sees that male-voice flagon, sing to the twisted barrier-rail.
'Cŵm Rhondda' and 'Penmachno' – hymns of yesterday –
Only half-remembered, I wonder what He'll say.

When He sees those touch-line tenors, with their copies made of sand:
Ten thousand instant Christians, and the Glynneath Silver Band.
'Come on mun, Ref., for Christ sake, that ball was still in play,'
Ten thousand instant Christians, I wonder what He'll say.

When He sees that empty chapel with its locked and shuttered doors,
And sees that dusty bible, cobwebbed-covered floors.
The numbers slowly dwindling, much fewer now each day:
Calfaria now a bingo-hall, I wonder what He'll say.

# Duw It's Hard

by Max Boyce

In our little valley they've closed the colliery down,
And the pithead baths is a supermarket now.
Empty journeys red with rust rolled to rest amidst the dust
And the pithead baths is a supermarket now.

CHORUS:
'Cos it's hard, Duw it's hard.
It's harder than they will ever know.
And it's they must take the blame:
The price of coal's the same,
But the pithead baths is a supermarket now.

They came down here from England because our output's low –
Brief-cases full of bank clerks that have never been below.
And they'll close the valley's oldest mine, pretending that they're sad.
But don't you worry, Butty bach, we're really very glad.

My clean-clothes-locker's empty now, I've thrown away the key.
And I've sold my boots and muffler and my lamp-check one-five-three.
But I can't forget the times we had, the laughing midst the fear,
'Cos every time I cough I get a mining souvenir.

I took my old helmet home with me, filled it full of earth.
And I planted little flowers there, they grew for all they're worth.
And it's hanging in the glass-house now – a living memory,
Reminding me they could have grown in vases over me.

But I know the local magistrate, she's got a job for me
Though it's only counting buttons in the local factory.
We get coffee breaks and coffee breaks, coffee breaks and tea,
And now I know those dusty mines have seen the last of me.

'Cos it's hard, Duw it's hard.
It's harder than they will ever know.
And if ham was underground would it be twelve bob a pound,
The pithead baths is a supermarket now.
Aye, the pithead baths is a supermarket now.

# Hymns and Arias

by Max Boyce

CHORUS:
And we were singing hymns and arias,
'Land of my Fathers', 'Ar hyd y nos'.

We paid our weekly shilling for that January trip:
A long weekend in London, aye, without a bit of kip.
There's a seat reserved for beer by the boys from Abercarn:
There's beer, pontoon, crisps and fags and a croakin' 'Calon Lan'.

Into Paddington we did roll with an empty crate of ale.
Will has lost at cards and now his Western Mail's for sale.
But Will is very happy though his money all has gone:
He swapped five photos of his wife for one of Barry John.

We told the guard that we're from Wales, and asked 'Is Twickers far?'
He said 'You can catch a 48 man, but it isn't very far.'
On the bus were boys from Blaina who'd been to see the Queen,
So we had a quick Gymanfa, aye, it was the greatest London's seen.

We got to Twickers early and were jostled in the crowd;
Planted leeks and dragons, looked for toilets all around.
So many there we couldn't budge – twisted legs and pale:
I'm ashamed we used a bottle that once held bitter ale.

*'. . . So we gave him that bottle, that once held bitter ale . . .'*
(HYMNS AND ARIAS)

Wales defeated England in a fast and open game.
We sang 'Cŵm Rhondda' and 'Delilah', damn, they sounded both the same.
We sympathized with an Englishman whose team was doomed to fail.
So we gave him that old bottle, that once held bitter ale!

He started singing hymns and arias,
'Land of my Fathers', 'Ar hyd y nos'.

So it's down to Soho for the night, to the girls with the shiny beads;
To the funny men with lipstick on, with evil minds and deeds.
One said to Will from a doorway dark, damn, she didn't have much on.
But Will knew what she wanted, aye ... his photo of Barry John!
And she was singing hymns and arias,
'Land of my Fathers', 'Ar hyd y nos'.

*'So it's down to Soho for the night, to the girls with the shining beads'*

# I Wandered Lonely

by Max Boyce

I wandered lonely through the crowd
With tired and aching feet.
Ticketless, and down in heart
Where ere I chanced to meet
A man with kindness in his eyes
Who said 'I got a spare.'
I thanked him there down on my knees
And I asked him 'But from where?'

He told me then the saddest tale
Of how his wife and he
Were two debenture holders
(North Stand, Block A, Row D).
But since his wife's dear mother died
Oh, she hasn't been the same
And she doesn't feel like going now.
(And I thought 'What a shame!')

So then I asked 'But why pick on me?
Don't the family want to go?'
He said 'They do, but the kick off's at three
And the funeral's ten to four!'

# Slow – Men at Work

by Max Boyce

There is a band of loyal men
Who come in their lorries but they don't say when.
What they do, well I just can't say –
They're either coming or they're going away.

CHORUS:
And they keep their billy-cans brewing,
They keep their billy-cans brewing.
They keep their billy-cans brewing
And they brew a little more each day!

But it's a dangerous job both cruel and hard;
They risk their lives when the floods are bad.
One drowned last week whilst clutching his spade:
He slipped and he fell in the tea he'd made!

Have you seen them working on the road,
Sweating and toiling with a heavy load?
Seen them working with no thought of tea?
Well if you have you don't live by me!

They say that Rome wasn't built in a day,
And there was one big long delay,
The reason was and it's a fact,
The council had the main contract!

*'. . . and they keep their billy-cans brewing . . .'*
(SLOW – MEN AT WORK)

# Rhondda Grey

by Max Boyce

One afternoon from a council school
A boy came home to play.
With paints and coloured pencils
And his homework for the day.
'We've got to paint the valley, Mam,
For Mrs Davies' art.
What colour is the valley, Mam?
And will you help me start?'

'Shall I paint the Con. Club yellow,
And paint the Welfare blue?
Paint old Mr Davies red
And all his pigeons too?
Paint the man who kept our ball –
Paint him looking sad?
What colour is the valley, Mam?
What colour is it Dad?'

'Dad, if Mam goes down the shop
To fetch the milk and bread,
Ask her fetch me back some paint –
Some gold and white and red.
Ask her fetch me back some green,
(The bit I've got's gone hard).
Ask her fetch me back some green;
Ask her, will you Dad?'

His father took him by the hand
And they walked down Albion Street.
Down past the old Rock Incline.
To where the council put a seat.

*'Rhondda Grey'*

Where old men say at the close of day
' 'Dy'n ni wedi g'neud ein siâr'*
And the colour in their faces says
'The tools are on the bar.
The tools are on the bar.'

'And that's the colour that we want
That no shop has ever sold.
You can't buy that in Woolies, lad,
With your reds and greens and gold.
It's a colour you can't buy, lad,
No matter what you pay.
But that's the colour that we want:
It's a sort of Rhondda Grey.'

'It's a colour you can't buy, lad,
No matter what you pay.
But that's the colour that we want:
They call it Rhondda Grey.
They call it Rhondda Grey.'

* We've done our share

# Sospan Fach

Mae bys Mari Ann wedi brifo
A Dafydd y gwâs ddim yn iach.
Mae'r baban yn y crud yn crio,
A'r gath wedi scrapo Johnny bach!
  SOSPAN FACH yn berwi ar y tân,
  Sospan fawr yn berwi ar y llawr,
  A'r gath wedi scrapo Johnny bach!

Mae bys Mari Ann wedi gwella
A Dafydd y gwâs yn ei fedd.
Mae'r baban yn y crud wedi tyfu,
A'r gath wedi huno mewn hedd!
  SOSPAN FACH yn berwi ar y tân,
  Sospan fawr yn berwi ar y llawr,
  A'r gath wedi scrapo Johnny bach!

Dai bach yn sowldiwr,
Dai bach yn sowldiwr,
Dai bach yn sowldiwr,
A gwt ei grys e'mas.

# Cŵm Rhondda

Wele'n sefyll rhwng y myrtwydd
Wrthrych teilwng o'm holl fryd:
Er mai o ran yr wy'n adnabod
Ei fod uwchlaw gwrthrychau'r byd:
Henffych fore
Y caf ei weled fel y mae.

Rhosyn Saron yw ei enw,
Gwyn a gwridog, teg o bryd;
Ar ddeng mil y mae'n rhagori
O wrthrychau penna'r byd:
Ffrind pechadur,
Dyma'r llywydd ar y môr.

Beth sydd imi mwy a wnelwyf
Ag eilunod gwael y llawr?
Tystio'r wyf nad yw eu cwmni
I'w gystadlu â m Iesu mawr:
O! am aros
Yn ei gariad ddyddiau f'oes.

MAX BOYCE's L.P.s are available from your local record dealer.

All the songs in this PANTHER BOOK are recorded by Max on either:

'MAX BOYCE "LIVE" AT TREORCHY' EMI ONE-UP OU 2033

'WE ALL HAD DOCTORS' PAPERS . . .' EMI MB 101

or

'MAX BOYCE IN SESSION' CAMBRIAN MCT 207

They are published by:

LAND OF SONG MUSIC. 41 Stirling Road, St Fagan's Court Estate, CARDIFF, South Wales.

AMBLESIDE MUSIC LTD. 21 Denmark Street, LONDON, WC2H 8NE.

CAMPBELL, CONNELLY & CO. LTD. 10 Denmark Street, LONDON WC2H 8LU.